The Torquay M
1853–1971

by
Frank Pearce

Frank Pearce writes not only from his knowledge as superintendent of the Marine Spa but as a well-known national and international author over many years. A World-War II veteran and twice a survivor from the Arctic convoys to Russia, his experiences led to several war documentaries, from one of which he was made a 'Fellow of the World Literary Academy' and the book awarded a place in the United States Senate Library. Among his latest subjects is local Devon history, with his most recent publication being *The Book of Torbay*.

OTHER TITLES BY THE AUTHOR

DOCUMENTARIES

The Ship That Torpedoed Herself
Last Call for HMS Edinburgh
Running the Gauntlet
Sea War
Heroes of the Fourth Service

CORNWALL TITLES

The High Kingdom
Falmouth to Helston
Brandy for the Parson
Portrait of a Cornish Village
Mayday, Mayday, Mayday
Along the Fal

DEVON TITLES

The Book of Torbay
The Book of Brixham

The Torquay Marine Spa
1853–1971

Copyright © Frank Pearce 2000

ORCHARD PUBLICATIONS
2   Orchard Close, Chudleigh, Newton Abbot, Devon TQ13 0LR
Telephone: (01626) 852714

ISBN 1 89896440 8

Printed by:
Hedgerow Print, Lapford, Crediton, Devon EX17 6AE

Contents

Page No.

Introduction – The Marine Spa 1

The Bath's Saloons 6

The Leander Club 23

King George V Reviews the Home Fleets 31

The New Marine Spa Swimming Bath 34

The Devon Arts Ball 41

The Torquay Rowing Club 47

Apprehension over the Swimming Bath and the Unfortunate Events
Preceding its Demolition 56

Acknowledgements

I am greatly indebted to the following for their co-operation, support and picture
contributions which have made this rare and unique history of the Spa possible.

Ann Blatchford	Torquay Leander Swimming Club
Richard Cudmore	Torquay Rowing Club
Max Danby	Flair Photography
Elsie Lamacraft	Formerly of Torquay Marine Spa
David Mason	Photographs
Robert Margetts	Torquay Leander Swimming Club
Mike Thompson	Herald Express
Phyllis Williams	for her special contribution
Phyllis White	Formerly of Torquay Marine Spa

INTRODUCTION – THE MARINE SPA

This book with its many photographs and literary recollections has been compiled principally as an evocative record of one of Torquay's most memorable monuments of pleasure and entertainment since the turn of the 20th Century – the Marine Spa.

That date has not been chosen as a convenient milestone but because at the dawn of this new Millennium, the years between, present the most reasonable threshold of living memory. Few people alive today remember the years preceding the 1914–1918 Great War. There are however, many who will recall the stories told them by their grandparents or dimly the events and places in their own lifetime. The last one hundred years is an ocean upon which for some period of time we have all sailed. We remember its capricious moods, its storms and calms, its ups and downs, the pleasures along the way, the company with whom we travelled.

Among this panoply of memoirs will surely be the resurrection of some personal memories of Torquay's Marine Spa. Although it has long since disappeared and only an ugly slab of stone marks its grave, we should not consider it as entombed memorabilia, for history is alive as we ourselves are and if we cease to search, to learn and to cherish these rare episodes, we are guilty of ingratitude to those who strove to create them. We also not only impoverish our own lives but deprive the inheritance of those who come after us. Today is the product of yesterday and tomorrow will be the product of today. History is now.

Moreover, not only are events a part of each other and of history but are also a part of larger events, each one sending out its ripples over the ocean of years, some to rebound and remind us that history is recurrent. Nostalgia is precious, is kind, but if, as so often happens, it is blurred by the mists of time, we tend to create myths and legends to suit the needs of our imagination, tottering on the brink of fantasy. That in turn can develop into a momentum of its own, startling even to reality. The dawn of the 20th century and the close of Victoria's reign, was for the most part and for the man in the street, a period of peaceful co-existence but today we live in an incessant uproar of violence about violence and in danger of knowing 'almost nothing' about 'almost everthing'.

The un-event has begun to be preferred to the event, fiction to fact. We strive to escape from a reality which terrifies us and are beset by dangers from which our ancestors, even our grandfathers, were relatively free, and like the effects of a slow insidious poison, have come to value the vulgar above the virtuous. To have something to write about to sell their papers, journalists resurrect great figures of our history, analyse their deeds and with their vitriolic pens take pride and pleasure in presenting an epitaph of character assassination.

In this digest of Torquay's beloved Marine Spa, the book draws attention to the esteem and admiration with which this beautiful building was held. From its uncertain beginnings and humble origins the Spa grew in stature and affection to become the focal point of Torquay life. The words 'Torquay' and 'Marine Spa' became as closely allied to one another as 'Horse and Carriage' or 'Gin and Tonic'.

Over the years it developed into a peninsular of entertainment, of conferences and comfortable leisure. Its position, poised on a jutting beacon, brooding over the huge natural harbour of Torbay made it unique, an establishment throbbing with life and vitality. Its history could never be compiled in terms of dull facts and figures, of meaningless inscriptions upon the barren grave it now is. Neither can it be left for future generations to stare at and speculate on the human stories and events that took place in the building that once graced this prime site. That indeed would be dishonourable to its memory, an act of culpable injustice.

This book with its encapsulated pictures and text, attempts to revive lost recollections, resurrect dim images of long ago and replace fantasy with fact, legend with literality. In the matter of legend, it touches upon some of the undercurrents of a crucial century reaching to the new millennium in which the tides of war and the tides of history turned together and the seeds of a new highly technical future were sown.

This photo of the Marine Spa in 1930 was taken from the higher level of Beacon Hill terrace and shows the highly popular 200 feet long Vita glass sun lounge overlooking Torbay. Immediately above it can be seen the twelve tall windows of the ballroom.

It is the century in which Britain found herself virtually caught between two kinds of civilization and, striving not to commit herself to a choice, finally drifted into a position from which she has never fully recovered, for she is neither European nor American.

While Torquay may have justifiably earned the soubriquet the 'English Riviera' equally so did the Marine Spa as 'Queen of the English Riviera'. She was not just a legend supported by fantasies, melodramatised by capricious memory; she was in fact a legend in her own lifetime, sustained by her unceasing popularity and undeniable beauty.

People of all colours and culture flirted with the Riviera Queen but while she generously bestowed her favours she fiercely defended her virtues and no one disputed her conquests.

This commanding and comprehensive view of the Spa shows Haldon Pier and in the foreground a peep of the ever popular Beacon Cove.

Because of its vantage point immediately overlooking the Bay, the Bath's Saloons had close links with all Marine activities and with those who go down to the sea in ships and have their business in great waters. Here in Torbay with its fascinating features, many Royal personages and titled notables disembarked from their yachts under the windows and balconies of the building in order to visit and to pay homage to this Queen of the English Riviera.

In this upper picture dated 1821, the artist shows the Strand on the extreme left, and centre, the long line of buildings now known as Victoria Parade. The hill on the extreme right is the site on which the Bath's Saloons (later known as the Marine Spa) was eventually built. The lower picture shows a close-up of the promontory site on which the building was erected 1850–1853.

From an old drawing of 1800, this was the viewpoint as seen from where the Imperial Hotel now stands. Beacon Cove can just be seen below the cliffs.

THE BATH'S SALOONS.

The origin of the old Bath's Saloons can be said to go back long before it was ever built, back to 1817 when people began to take an interest in swimming as a health pastime. That year, a certain Dr Pollard built a bath of sorts on the site of what is now the Regina Hotel on Victoria Parade by the harbour. It was known as the Bath House at that time. When in 1929, builders were excavating in order to instal a lift, some of the old bath was found under the drawing room.

An interesting story emerges from this old Bath House, for in 1838 Elizabeth Barrett Browning stayed there for health reasons, but a tragedy marred the good results of her visit. Her brother E.M.Barrett who was staying with her went for a cruise in Babbacombe Bay on July 11th, 1840, in a boat called La Belle Savage. With him were Captain Clarke, a man named Vanneck and a boatman William White. When two or three miles off Teignmouth the boat capsized in a squall, all being drowned. Captain Clarke's and William White's bodies were recovered, Clarke's body being brought in a week later by the two sons of the Reverend Francis Lyte (famed for his hymn 'Abide with me') of Brixham. Although they are buried in Torre churchyard, no stone marks their resting place. Elizabeth Barrett's letters written during her stay in Torquay show that although almost bed-ridden at the time, she did much literary work. She left Torquay in September 1841, the journey to London being in a patent carriage with a bed in which 'is to waft us through the air upon a thousand springs'. It was during the first year of Miss Barrett's residence here that Tennyson paid a visit to 'the loveliest sea village in England'. The Regina Hotel still exists in Victoria Parade.

The picture (right) was taken in 1908 and shows the unveiling of a plaque affixed to the wall of the Regina Hotel at the bottom of Beacon Hill to the memory of Elizabeth Barrett Browning On the right is Lady Newnes and on the left Councillor Iredale owner of a large bookshop on the Strand adjacent to Shapley's Grocery Store. Next is Mr J.M.Scott, Manager of the Bath's

Saloons and standing next to the plaque is the former Mayor of Torquay, Councillor E.H.Sermon, owner of a prestigious jeweller's shop in Victoria Parade.

By 1852, the requirements of the town had outgrown the bathing capabilities

of Dr Pollard's Bath House and in August, a company was formed to erect new baths on Beacon Hill. The shares were readily taken up by those who thought the undertaking would benefit the town as a health resort and in September 1853 the front of the high ground of Beacon Hill was removed to obtain the necessary space for the building as seen in the picture below.

This shows the Beacon promontory on which the Bath's saloons were established. In the lower right hand corner is a glimpse of Shaw's Shipbuilding Yard.

The planned project would include a large saloon or hall which might provide facilities for concerts, debates, conferences, dances or even a roller skating-rink, also facilities for private baths. Beneath this complex would be a large swimming bath with open arches to the sea.

The foundation stone of the Bath's Saloons complex was laid by the daughter of Sir Lawrence Palk in 1830 and the face of the hill partially cut away by 1853. Later the rest of the promontory was removed for the completion of the building and to provide material with which to construct Haldon Pier which enclosed some ten acres of water to form the harbour. This being completed in August 1870, its formal opening happened to coincide with that year's Torbay Royal Regatta.

To mark the occasion, Sir Lawrence Palk offered a 100 guineas cup for a Channel race from Cowes to Torquay, and the Yacht Clubs offered similar prizes which resulted in a magnificent muster of yachts in Torbay. Following the declaration of the opening of the harbour on August 20th, 1870, the townspeople gave a grand

Shaw's Shipbuilding Yard. Towering above it are the Bath's Saloons Reading Rooms where Charles Dickens entertained large audiences.

dinner in the large saloon inviting all the yacht owners and upwards of 450 gentlemen to dine together. The construction of the new harbour being looked upon as a wonderful benefit to the town. The inhabitants presented Sir Palk with a portrait of himself at a cost of £125. On August 24th, Sir Palk and his family were invited to a banquet in the new saloon where the portrait presentation was made.

The inscription ran – 'Presented to Sir Lawrence Palk, Bart. MP by his friends at Torquay and Haldon as a mark of esteem and regard in commemoration of the construction by him of the new harbour 1870'.

At around 1855, the Ladies Bathing Cove (Beacon Cove) was enlarged and a breakwater erected to form a defence against rough seas but this was swept away by a severe gale in 1859.

The swimming bath under the Bath's Saloons, with open archways to the sea, was opened in August 1857 but although it was an important asset to the town it was never a financial success.

The company was badly advised and met with so many obstacles and had such an ever increasing debt, it was agreed that it should be wound up with the liability standing at £13,000. As a result, the shareholders lost not only what they had invested but were called upon to contribute towards paying off the debt.

In that same year (1857) Britain and America were united by the Atlantic cable. So it remained until December 1862 when it was sold to Mr W. Kitson and others for £3,500, and the company wound up in May 1863. A new era opened later when the quarrying of Beacon Hill for the construction of Haldon Pier opened up space for building stores on the quay. On the left of the building marked 'Baths Reading Rooms' the picture opposite shows a piece of the old hill before this too was removed and on the piece of flat ground below it shows 'Shaw's Ship-Building Yard' in 1856, which was later demolished. It was here in the Reading Rooms shown that Dickens entertained with readings from his literary works.

The second half of the nineteenth century was marked by a brilliant period of literary genius. Poetry was represented by Browning and Tennyson, prose by Macauley and Carlyle and novelism by Dickens and Thackery. Dickens (1812–1870) and Thackery (1815–1863) though contemporaries and rivals brought the novel of contemporary life to its highest development, but both also wrote historical novels. Dickens' strength lay mainly in caricature, sometimes grotesque, of middle-class life, and several of his novels attacked the evils of the day. His chief works were *Pickwick*, his first novel, and *David Copperfield*. They were gems of literary genius exposing the downtrodden conditions of the working classes.

Around 1862–1863 at the Bath's Saloons Reading Rooms, Charles Dickens entertained with two hour daily readings from his popular stories *Christmas Carol*, *Pickwick Papers*, *David Copperfield*, and *Nicholas Nickleby*. It was at this time that Dickens' stories in serial form were being published in the *New York Herald* and devotedly read by a large public. Among other tales was the *Old Curiosity Shop* relating the sad and dramatic story of the character 'Little Nell'. Such was the interest in his writings in the United States that on one of his visits to New York, hundreds of people waiting at the quayside bombarded him with the same question, "Did little Nell die?". This visit around the same period must have been a rather exciting time for Dickens, for it was then that Abraham Lincoln proclaimed the end of slavery. Three years later because of his belief in the rights of all mankind Lincoln was assassinated.

Thackery on the other hand satirized the vices and follies of high society, as he showed in his first and greatest novel *Vanity Fair*. Of many other eminent novelists of that period were Charlotte Bronte (1816–1855) whose prime work was Jane Eyre and Mary Anne Evans who wrote under the name of George Eliot. Chief among the novelists at the end of the century whose name is legion is Robert Louis Stevenson (1850–1894) particularly with his much loved *Treasure Island*. However much the latter part of the nineteenth century and the opening of the twentieth is to be complimented, they were not without their drawbacks. There was a feverish struggle after wealth, leading to a worship of money. Large cheap mechanical production ended in the death throes of artistic taste, and that, combined with the mammon of material prosperity, proved fatal to the highest forms of art in painting, literature and music.

This flood of commercialism walked hand in hand with the onset of the Industrial Revolution which began as early as the mid-18th century. Breeding was prolific, large families popular, with broods of six to ten children. In Victoria's reign alone from 1837 to 1901, the population of Britain doubled from 20 million to 40 million. The revolution changed the daily lives of millions of people and generally raised the standards of living.

Although Torquay was not an industrial centre, the circulation of increased wealth brought more and more people to seek and settle in more salubrious surroundings like Torbay. This is vividly shown in the census figures for Torquay and Paignton from 1851 to 1951. In 1851, the population of Torquay was just under 16,000 but one hundred years later 53,000. Paignton's rate of increase was even more rapid, rising in that same period from 4,000 to 25,000.

In the mid 1800s there emerged a body of devotees who were convinced that seawater possessed body-healing properties that could cure almost every ailment. At first this led to an obsession of sea-water bathing but later when medical science discovered that seaweed contained certain medicinal benefits, Spas and medical centres introduced Seaweed Baths. This treatment became highly popular among the faithful who later patronised the Bath's Saloons Medical Department in their hundreds. Other favourites among the forty different treatments offered were mud baths, peat baths, vapour baths, brine baths and needle baths. These latter were circular frames of narrow chrome-plated tubes punctured by thousands of tiny holes. The patient stood in the centre while powerful jets of varied temperatured water were injected on the body.

The effect was similar to a thousand needles piercing the skin and although smarting at first, the end result was highly exhilarating. The patient felt he had overcome gravity.

From records in the Torquay Directory of 1860, it played an important part in

the life of the community as this letter of 1859 suggests –
'Dear Sir,

   We beg to call attention to the advantages which that splendid establishment offers during the winter season and trust that the support which is so well deserved may be given both by residents and visitors so as to enable the Governors to carry out their designs not only in providing first rate baths but a promenade unequalled in salubrity and beauty in the magnificent saloon and terrace. Cold and tepid, fresh or seawater plunge, vapour, douche and every description of baths are always in readiness, and visitors have access to the reading room and library which also contains many new works.'

   It would seem that prior to the availability of the Bath's Saloons, even wealthy households in Torquay relied on hip baths in front of the bedroom fire.

   In 1887 there was much criticism about the exit arrangements from the foyer of the Bath's Saloons after dances and gala ball occasions, especially on cold, wet winter nights. Plans were drawn up for a large outside porch to be built where patrons could wait for carriages to arrive in the quagmire of the yard outside. After all, it was argued, not all ladies had the assistance of a 'footman'. However, objections to the porch were many pointing out that if this were built it would greatly restrict the turning space for horses.

The cab rank at Wellswood, Torquay, in 1890, typical of that which would have formed outside the Bath's Saloons Ballroom.

   But the closing days of the horse and carriage were fast approaching with the advent of the new means of transport, the motor-car. With the establishment of this new mobility, the restricted turning space outside the proposed porch would cause no problem.

Although the period of the Bath's Saloon's ballroom hey-days correspond with the debut of the motor-car which replaced the horse and carriage, one can hardly imagine titled personages from the Higher Lincombes and Higher Warberrys leaving the ballroom after a festive occasion to climb into a menial 'Tin Lizzie', no matter how dark the night. If at that time they had become the proud owner of a super-car, it would surely have been one of the more elegant models.

As far as women's fashions were concerned, this was the period when they were enduring the agony of the infamous whalebone, the tyranny of restrictive corsetry. For the rich, clothes were the status symbol of social advantage, marking their superior position over the poor. Nowhere was this more apparent than at the saloon functions when banquets and balls were the highlights of the social merry-go-round, especially in that year of 1887 when Queen Victoria's Diamond Jubilee was being celebrated with much enthusiasm.

Whilst the Saloons were the meeting place of the titled and well-off, there is no doubt there were certain needy areas in Torquay, for records show that infrequent festivities were occasioned 'to feed the poor'.

In those early days the Saloon's great room was constantly used for a variety of public meetings, the most unusual being a religious mission in 1880 which was

The beautiful Spa Ballroom was the focal point of Torbay's social life. The tall windows on the right behind the bandstand faced out onto Beacon Cove and lower right are two of the several glass doors leading out into the Vita glass sun lounge.

well attended. It was organised by an order of monks led by a certain Father Ignatious. Unfortunately, the generous collection from it, which had been transferred to Llanthony Abbey for safe keeping was also generously collected by thieves who broke into the Abbey and got clean away.

Lord Haldon (1818–1883)

Torquay suffered a great loss in March 1883 when after a period of illness, its great benefactor Lord Haldon died. As Sir Lawrence Palk, M.P., he bestowed a large part of his fortune on the improvement of the town in many ways and especially the conversion and extension of the saloon's building.

At around the turn of the century, women were asserting their right to vote in Parliamentary elections. The movement led by a militant activist Mrs Emiline Pankhurst earned itself the name of 'suffragettes'. Although the weight of their campaign was in the big cities, especially London, it had a strong following in Torquay. A protest meeting was held at the Bath's Saloons in support of the movement attended by a large company of women in the great room. Although the police tried to break up the demonstration, they were outnumbered and the meeting developed into a 'free for all'. The constables stood no chance against the onslaught of those dreaded weapons, the 'black gamp' and the 'whirling handbag'.

On the south side of the Spa's foyer was the cooling lounge, 44 feet by 38 feet and 20 feet high, where people could rest after their treatment in the medical section. It was a beautiful room with its ceiling and walls embellished with rich pale blue and gilt moulded reliefs. The ladies and gentlemen's wings also provided seven treatment areas with fifteen dressing rooms.

The main entrance hall or foyer (as shown in the photograph overleaf) was an architectural feature in itself with its beautifully designed balcony, elaborate ornamental inner wall buttresses and elegant cupolated dome. The wide doorway opposite with two of the permanent medical staff led to the cooling house.

In 1894 at a cost of £22,000 (which had to be borrowed) electric lighting machinery was installed in the cellars under the roadway in front of the entrance to the Bath's Saloons. Unfortunately during these operations a workman was killed by a falling girder.

The Foyer

The palm laden foyer of 1899. Beyond it, partly hidden, can be seen the interior of the cooling lounge.

The original Ballroom which in later years was used as a cooling lounge as part of the medical section.

A proposal to attract more visitors was made by the mayoress in September 1899 and as a result the great room and foyer was partly filled with palms and plants to make it into a sort of Palm Court. However, it seems that so much room was taken up by this florestation it left little room for other activities. One irate critic's letter to the press clearly expresses his opinion: "This heap of bark and withered greenery is a transparent attempt on popular credulity in this silly venture". The palms were removed forthwith.

When Britain took her first few faltering steps into the 20th century, she discovered it was not the quiescent comfortable world the Empire orientated poets of the Victorian era had predicted and over which they had eulogised with endless prose. Instead, there were uncertain paths bestrewn with unexpected problems. Great as had been the general progress in the old Queen's reign it had not been without its drawbacks. The feverish struggle after wealth had led to a worship of money. Railways and telegraphs had imparted an impatient rush to keep pace with modern life.

Availability of cheap rail fares allowed the less well-off from the industrial areas of England, Scotland, the Midlands and London to travel to Torbay to enjoy the advantages of its warm climate and panoramic beauty. The two pictures opposite show the very early days of rail travel in 1822 on the Manchester to Liverpool line and the same station eight years later in 1830.

Cheap mechanical production was proving fatal to former excellence of quality and the sudden increase in mining and factory building was disfiguring the countryside. Most serious of all Germany, led by Kaiser Wilhelm was rapidly increasing her navy thus imposing a threat to Britain's control of her trade routes on which she so much depended. The new wonders of advancing science like electricity, the motor car, Marconi's wireless and the aeroplane were having a deleterious effect on the dying breed of die-hard Victorians who were convinced that all these new-fangled ideas would eventually disappear. The dawn of the new century revealed a whole package of new ideas and inventions which were commercially developed to form the nucleus of trade expansion. The spin-off from this was reflected in gradually improved living conditions; firstly in the big cities and later in country areas and seaside resorts. In the wake of this evolution, the effect, though slow at first, gained a momentum with the velocity of its pace steadily increasing. The dawns of new horizons were appearing, new pleasures and new opportunities to be grasped.

Among these was the exciting experience of a holiday by the sea; where better than Torquay with the splendour of its coastal scenery? As better industrial conditions developed so its popularity as a seaside resort grew, especially in the bank holiday periods when the town's population could double overnight. Here were the beaches, the walks, the scenery and, if it rained, an hour or two at the Bath's Saloons (later known as the Marine Spa) providing morning music in comfortable, relaxed conditions.

Among the many renowned artistes who gave performances in the Bath's Saloons was the world renowned pianist Paderewski. His visit here in 1894 brought huge crowds to listen to his rendering of the works of Beethoven, Liszt, Schubert and Mozart. The prices of tickets were 10/6 and 5/–. The performance received acclaim from those present but apparently not like the wild exhibitions that took place in Glasgow when at the close of the maestro's performance he was so enthusiastically mobbed by his audience with floral tributes, his hands were almost shaken off and even devotedly kissed. There was however, an unfortunate sequel to Paderewski's visit, for a year later in 1895, Paish Ltd, who owned a large music shop took it upon themselves to hire the large saloon and booked Paderewski for a return performance. Probably, acting in the best interest of the public, Paish, reduced the former 10/6 tickets to 5/–. At Plymouth, where the pianist was to visit first, tickets were sold at 5/–, 2/6 and 1/–. Apparently, Paderewski took exception to these price reductions, judging it demeaned the dignity of the occasion. As a result he refused to honour his booking at either Torquay or Plymouth and returned forthwith to London. The anger and frustration was passionate, for many had travelled long distances to these venues at considerable expense to hear the genius of the great man playing. For many weeks, letters poured into the offices of the Torquay Directory with biting condemnation of the pianist's action. Some time later in an effort to try to justify his decision he wrote the following letter–

"It is said I objected to playing before an audience which had only paid five shillings. Not at all. I have often played to a shilling audience but one doesn't put Torquay on the same level as Manchester for instance. I objected to the price being reduced in Torquay and being advertised by the local agent as though he had hired me."

The loss to Paish must have been considerable for it was said that for a tour of seventy concerts Paderewski was able to command a fee of £36,000, a sum of money never before reached by any instrumentalist. Although Paish Ltd tried to persuade the council to reimburse the money they had invested for the hire of the Bath's Saloons hall, the application failed.

The Torquay Directory however, seemed unimpressed by the audiences reaction to Paderewski's concert in 1894, "Although Torquay audiences are somewhat phlegmatic" they said, "and are usually prone to exercise a reserve which is at once icy and depressing, frigidity was entirely lacking from this performance". It was not exactly a glowing tribute of the audience's appreciation. Was this a sober reflection of how local audiences normally reacted to other great audiences of that period? For instance at the nearby Torquay Pavilion, such virtuosos as Mark Hamburg, Dame Nellie Melba, Sir Henry Wood and Sir Edward Elgar frequently performed. One wonders, if audience appreciation was equally low key?

Above is a copy of the front pages of No. 1 and No. 24 of the Torquay directories dated 1839 and 1840. The first coinciding closely with Queen Victoria's accession to the throne and the second with her marriage to Prince Albert.

Below are reproductions of two editors of the Torquay Directory. The first in 1839 is of Mr Edward Cockrem and the second Mr G.H. Lidstone in 1939.

In the years prior to Queen Victoria's death in 1901, several important events took place at the Bath's Saloons. For instance in 1888, tennis tournaments were arranged in the great room which was being used as a skating rink, and records show that in 1878, members of Thomas Eddison's staff demonstrated to an awestruck audience the miracle of the phonograph or talking machine, later known as the gramophone. At the end of the lecture the wonder instrument was activated producing recordings of speech and music through a funnel, the sound of which, though somewhat metallic, delighted the huge audience.

Little wonder it created so much interest, for the Torquay Directory of 1876 carried the news that a man called Alexander Graham Bell had invented a gadget called a telephone by which means people could speak to one another over variable distances through a wire. Some shook their heads in wonderment, what was the world coming to they argued. Others thought it had all the hallmarks of devilry.

In 1890, the Princess Louise and her escort the Marquis of Lorne visited Torquay to open an Arts and Crafts Exhibition at the Saloons. The introduction of gas jet lighting in 1891 had a mixed reception for although the better lighting was appreciated, the effect of seventy jets, each consuming as much oxygen as six adults with all the doors and windows closed, left the audience with violent headaches and nausea.

In March 1901, a young man stood at the rostrum in the great room of the Bath's Saloons and gave a fascinating lecture on his experiences as a War correspondent during the Boer War in South Africa. His name was Winston

Churchill then aged twenty-five. Thirty nine years later he was to become Britain's Prime Minister and its greatest war leader in the nation's history. Even at that early age, the eloquence of his oratory held the crowded audience spellbound.

No less captivated were the crowds who came to the Spa to listen to the dynamic playing of the famous violinists Kreisler and Kubelik. These were occasions when the ballroom was filled to capacity, often with standing room only.

When such a celebrity as Dame Clara Butt gave performances between the years 1900 to 1906, her magnificent voice also kept audiences spellbound. By comparision there were what can only be described as presentations of 'quack healing'. The variety of so called miracle healings claimed was astonishing: deafness, paralysis, defective eyesight, rheumatism, gout, stiff joints, neuralgia, lumbago, sciatica, even stuttering. In fact as George said in Jerome's book *Three Men in a Boat* everything except housemaid's knee.

In the years 1924 to 1928, the public began to take a more lively interest in the activities at the Marine Spa complex. The ballroom, attractively decorated, enticed more people to its dances and other functions than it had for some time. Dance competitions, association parties, club functions and carnivals gave an enormous boost to the finances. The town's social life was targeted on this centre of entertainment. The beautiful Vita glass sun lounge was an added attraction where visitors and residents could relax and be served with tea or coffee and listen to the adjoining ballroom orchestra's music. This lounge was the largest in Great Britain at the time with magnificent sea views overlooking Beacon Cove with all its swimming activities. To combat condensation problems, rows of electric lights and lamps were fitted and a maple floor laid over an underfloor of deal. Access to the ballroom from the sun lounge was provided through two pairs of double doors each fitted with bevelled plate glass. Separate access and exit at the western end of the sun lounge led to the medical section.

The improvement was undoubtedly due to the arrival of a new figure in the person of Mr Berkeley Hollyer who, having relinquished his post as Manager of Droitwich Spa, took over the responsibility of the Spa complex in 1931 as General Manager and Publicity Officer of Torquay involving the correlation and publication of the Torquay Guide from Mr Scott. His drive and vigorous personality was responsible for several changes in the running of the Spa which brought added and welcome revenue. It was at about this period that the title of Bath's Saloons was replaced by 'Torquay Marine Spa'.

The Torquay Marine Spa Vita glass sun lounge, 1933.

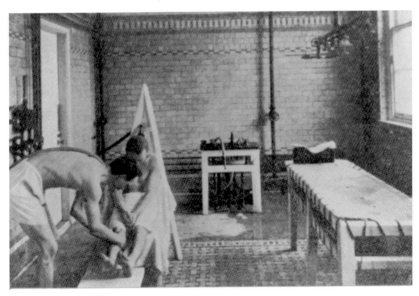

One of the treatment rooms at the Spa Medical Baths.

The fully qualified staff at the Saloons, under the control and supervision of the joint Superintendents Mr Hooper and Miss Hardacre, were constantly being updated and supplied with the latest in electrical equipment which established the department as one of the most advanced in the country.

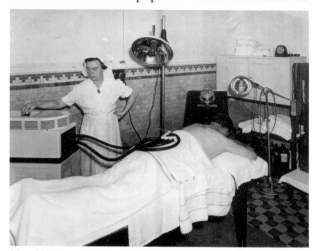

Miss Hardacre applies elictrical therapy to a patient.

Following the turbulence and suffering of World War II from 1939 to 1945, the fruits of peace were slow in coming. People were still dependant on the ration book issue for food, clothing and petrol. Gradually, so very gradually, the country settled down to a more liberal existence. But one thing was clear, life would never be the same again. The people were on the march. Changes were taking place in the life pattern; new and exciting ideas were emerging; patience and tolerance disappearing; the pace of life faster and faster. People wanted things done yesterday, not today.

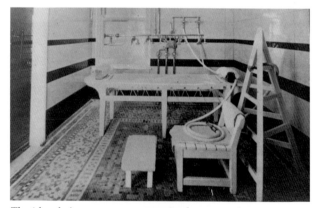

The 'douche' treatment room awaits the next patient.

With the advent of the Queen's Coronation in 1953 it was another opportunity for celebration. Many buildings were floodlit and the Marine Spa provided a grand celebration. During the daytime several conferences took place in the ballroom where its elegant and stately surroundings were much appreciated by delegates. For one of the larger functions in 1954, the far end balcony was removed to be replaced by the existing band-stand. This was to accommodate the famous Ted Heath's London Band with its complement of top musicians.

THE LEANDER CLUB

The little cove adjacent to the Bath's Saloons known as Beacon Cove during the late 1800s was set aside for ladies only. Mixed bathing had been strictly forbidden from early times. To provide a sense of privacy to bathing belles at the cove, bushes and a high fence were established on the high ground overlooking the beach to hide the gaze of inquisitive males. On seats just above the cove were notices to the effect they were not to be occupied by males during the hours of bathing and this was supported by an occasional police patrol. In fact, a man named Bill Ford was employed by the council as a guard to physically stop men from looking down on the ladies in the water. What they could have seen is a mystery, for the girls wore monstrous voluminous costumes virtually covering them from head to toe.

An early period etching view of Beacon Cove around 1820. It shows the forerunner of the later bathing machine. Whilst Beacon Cove was largely set aside for use by the general public, the Torquay Leander Swimming Club, in the early years, used the well known Peaked Tor beach some distance away, out of sight behind the rocky cliff face shown on the left of the picture.

In 1867, one very Victorian prudish gentleman wrote to the Torquay Directory to the effect that in his opinion the spectacle of ladies bathing was most unsightly. He then went on to propose that large barges should be anchored some distance off-shore with exits facing seaward and in a position where the bathers could be conveyed to and from Beacon Cove in small boats. Apparently the letter aroused no earth-shattering interest and this brilliant idea sank without trace.

In 1897 Torquay had a bye-law stating that –

'No person of the male sex shall at any time bathe within fifty yards of a ladies' bathing machine.'

Another view of Beacon Cove around the 1920s. This was before the modern cafe had been built.

Beacon Cove in 1936. On the right are the curved windows of the swimming bath and in the centre of the beach, the outlet pipe for the 95,000 gallons of water when the bath had to be emptied.

The Leander Club was formed as early as 1897 with a meeting at Haarer's Restaurant next to the old Burlington Cinema near the Post Office in Fleet Street. There, it was officially formed into the Torquay Leander Swimming and Life Saving Society and in the years that followed, right up to the present, its members have brought great honours to the town in the world of national and international swimming events. Among its founder members are the names of its secretary for over forty years, Bill Luscombe, also the great international diver Tack Collings and in company with these Torquay established names are Sydney Coombes, Charles Downey and Thomas Bond. They were the men who actually launched the society into its highly successful progression. Under the expert tuition of Tack Collings, members became most proficient in the art of diving. 'Tack' at this time was one of the finest trick divers in the country and in 1908 represented Great Britain in the Olympic Games in London.

At the Olympic games trials in Blackpool in 1928, Leander had six representatives. The youngest of the party, Gladys Luscombe, a schoolgirl at Torquay Girls Grammar School was selected. She became Torquay's second and youngest international star.

However, in the 1800s, there was very little coaching for swimming in Torquay. With very few facilities they did the best they could to teach one another. The swimming activities from the 1850s were confined to the small beach of Peaked Tor mentioned earlier.

'Tack' Collings in his famous swallow dive from 60ft Saddle rock at Peaked Tor, Torquay into only 6ft to 9ft of water.

The following picture shows the occasion of Leander's annual Christmas dip in the year 1906. There appear to be far more spectators than swimmers.

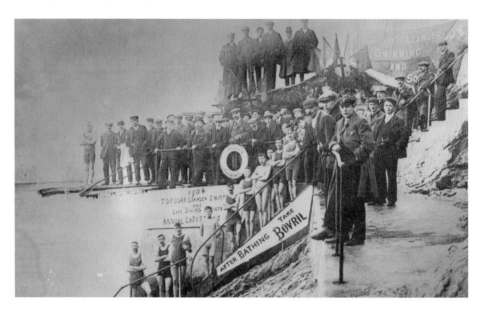

But this Leander Christmas dip of 1908 brought far more swimmers than spectators.

In 1948, a few of Leander's ladies' swimming team dressed up in the old fashioned bathing costumes of the late 1800s and early 1900s. This photo was taken in the Vita glass sun lounge of the Marine Spa. Six year old Julie Dunn was the Miss Future.

Among those in the photograph are – Pauline Heywood, Maureen Hayes, Glennis Phillips, Margaret Short, Audrey Weeks, Jean Hern, Mary Burridge, Shirley Cann, Geraldine Vinnicombe, Bernice Trodden, Monica Pearce, Christine Popman and little Julie Dunn.

Torquay Leander Swimming and Water Ballet.

The two main activities at the Spa Swimming Bath were competitive swimming and water ballet. In the former, Leander usually headed the championships list, in fact, during one season winning fourteen of the twenty County championship events. Water ballet started in 1948 under the production and direction of Frank Pearce and Stella Margetts. The shows comprised synchronised swimming to waltz music with coloured spotlights in opaque darkness, which attracted large audiences from all parts of the west between 1948 and 1960. It was an entirely new concept in swimming entertainment and Torquay Leander was probably the first club in Great Britain to introduce water ballet as it came to be known. The big night opened with a great deal of apprehension as to whether the show would be acceptable to the public. The scenic background was minimal, with the bath wall at the shallow end covered in tall bullrushes with twelve of the best girl swimmers emerging from four carefully constructed, enormous water-lilies. Each team of four swam in line, synchronising their strokes and in rhythmic timing with the music. That first trial show lasted its scheduled twenty minutes but when the music stopped there was a long silence. When it was realised the show was completed, the audience burst into applause, whistling and cheering. It was obvious the new show would have to be repeated. Little did the club realise they had committed themselves to putting on this and similar productions every summer for the next twelve years. That period was a very busy time for the Leander Club, for championship successes went hand in hand with water ballet presentations.

Torquay Leader's first water ballet show (1948). L. to R.: Audrey Baigent, Yvonne Schroeder, Jean Bullock, Jean Hern, Pauline Heywood, Margaret Short, Geraldine Vinnicombe, Glennis Phillips, Doris Bond, Kathleen Bond, Ann Margetts, Monica Pearce, Shirley Cann, Vanessa Marchant.

Opposite: Torquay Leader's water ballet team (1951–52). L. to R. (1st row): Jean Hearn, Irene Nicholls, Joan Hewitt, Vicky Cook, (unknown), Frank Pearce. (Middle row): Shirley Cann, Kathleen Bond. (Top row): Christine Pain, Audrey Sanders, (unknown), Yvonne Schroeder, Ann Newcombe, Audrey Weeks, Kathleen Bond, (unknown), (unknown).

Torquay Leader's first water ballet team (1948). L. to R. (sitting): Doris Bond, show producer and author Frank Pearce, Jean Hern. L. to R. (standing): Audrey Weeks, Monica Pearce, Stella Margetts, Glennis Phillips, Shirley Cann, Margaret Short. L. to R. (on steps) Jean Bullock, Ann Margetts, Geraldine Vinnicombe, Yvonne Schroeder, Vanessa Marchant.

In January 1997, Leander celebrated its 100th birthday at the Carlton Hotel, Torquay, with many members of the club being present to mark the occasion. The photograph below shows a similar event in January 1977 when Leander celebrated its 80th birthday, as Gordon Ley, the Devon County Amateur Swimming Association President, cut the decorated cake.

Left to right: Christine Margetts, Stella Margetts, Robert Margetts, Mrs McDonald, Mrs Alma Ley, Mr G. McDonald, Gordon Ley (President), Edward Dean (Western Counties President), Mrs Irene Dean, Ken Dennis and Mrs M. Dennis.

KING GEORGE V REVIEWS THE HOME FLEETS

In July 1910, Torbay was honoured by the arrival of the combined Atlantic, Mediterranean and Home fleets for a naval review by King George V. It was a magnificent sight with the presence of 230 warships including 37 large battleships. There were spectacular views from the windows of the Bath's Saloons.

The view of part of the anchored fleet as seen from the Bath's Saloons.

A splendid view of the Bath's Saloon's vantage point overlooking the anchored fleet. From the amount of smoke pouring out of the Spa's boiler room chimney it appears to be also preparing to go to sea.

The assembled fleets await review by King Gearge V in the Royal Yacht.

After the review the King comes ashore at Princess Pier to be met by the Mayor, Councillor C. Spragg and other dignitaries of the Torquay Borough Council.

A contrast in naval power. This shows Queen Victoria's review of the fleet in the Firth of Forth sixty-eight years earlier in 1842.

At the end of the week the King came ashore at the aptly named Princess Pier to return to London by train. He was met by the Mayor of Torquay, Councillor C.H. Spragg and other dignitaries of the Borough Council.

THE NEW MARINE SPA SWIMMING BATH

In 1910, the council decided it was necessary for the image of the town that a new swimming bath should be built. There were two main reasons for this forward thinking concept:

1. Swimming as an important contribution to good health was rapidly gaining ground in the country. The advantages of this exercise especially in sea water were publicised in countless national newspapers and magazines but unfortunately the cold temperatures of our coastal waters prohibited such activity for most of the year .
2. The old dark, sunless swimming bath under the Bath's Saloons, open to the destructive violence of sea storms was proving to be a failing and costly enterprise. Meanwhile, covered warm water swimming baths were springing up in many industrial towns and seaside resorts and Torquay as a favourite and popular holiday venue could not be seen to be left out of this euphoria of leisure attractions.

As a result of the council's decision it was proposed that the new modern bath should be sited at the head of the approach to Beacon Cove.

At that time it was thought the cost would be in the region of £6,000 (an unrealistic figure). However, after giving the matter further consideration, an application to borrow a more practical sum of £15,000 was made and approved. The lowest tender of £14,912 by E.P. Bovey was made and accepted but with the onset of World War I the start of the building was delayed for a while.

However, despite all the setbacks resulting from the war, such as shortage of labour, materials and rising prices, the building of the new swimming bath went ahead as planned. There were many protests about the increasing costs and the siting of the new bath, but the council continued with its objective. A supporter of the project wrote to the local paper as follows – "Why are people always grumbling, why is nothing ever right? Why don't they shake the dust of Torquay off their feet and try to find some other perfect place in which to live, that is if they can find one?".

By the end of 1915, costs had risen to between £17,000 and £20,000, and it was not until late 1916 that it was officially opened by the Mayor (Councillor Towell) to whom the architect presented a golden key.

From 1900 to 1920, with the availability of improved rail communication between the Midlands and the west Country, middle-class families settled in Torquay and, as a result, the aristocracy began moving out. The increase of a predominant middle-class population was not to the liking of some of Torquay's older generation and an example of their dissatisfaction was expressed in a letter to the Torbay Directory in 1909:–

"Sir, Torquay is not and never will be a place for trippers. Try to bring back the glories of the past, when all the large houses were occupied by the gentry, who brought their equipages and servants. It is pitiable to see most of which were formerly tenanted by gentry either converted into hotels or boarding houses or, still worse, empty. Everything has been done to drive the villa residents away".

If the aforesaid gentleman could have seen Torquay sands in the busy holiday periods of the future he would probably have collapsed. These were times when in the regular Midlands' industrial holiday fortnight in August the population increased by some 25,000.

Abbey Sands showing the collonaded shelter and cafe in the 1930s

The new swimming bath in the mid 1920s. This view taken from the diving boards end, shows on the right and at the shallow far end, the men's dressing cubicles. The ladies' cubicles are out of sight on the left. A spectator balcony extended around the whole length and breadth of the building. The bright area in the ceiling is the glass roof, and the trailing ropes from the balcony were used to adjust ceiling ventilation.

Torquay sands, 1925

Admission to the new swimming bath was quite reasonable even for those days: swim ticket sixpence, spectators twopence, loan of costume and towel fourpence. The overall swimming area was 90 feet in length and 30 feet in width with the water graduating from 4 feet 6 inches in the shallow end to 7 feet 6 inches at the deep end, serving three diving boards at heights of 4 feet, 8 feet and 12 feet respectively with the addition of a springboard 2 feet above water level. The floor and surround of the pool consisted of Italian non-slip Terrazo stone which was so levelled to allow drainage to run back. Dressing cubicles and two cloakrooms were provided for the ladies' and gentlemen's sections with toilets at the Beacon Cove end of the building. Upstairs, a spectator balcony ran around both sides and ends, allowing a large number of people to watch competitive galas and water polo contests.

In 1924 and 1926, slipper baths were installed on the balcony behind the spectator seating accommodation. At the diving boards end of the building three large parabolic windows looked out on to Beacon Cove.

Although in 1915 the bath had not been officially opened, the Torquay Leander Swimming and Life Saving Society were allowed the use of the bath for teaching of swimming and life saving. That was the first period when Leander used the pool as their headquarters. It was short lived, however, for in 1916 the bath was appropriated for the sole use of the men of the armed forces. The convenient flat area of the car park was also consigned to them for drill parades. However, just before the services took control that year, Leander held its first gala. With the men away, the ladies' section took on the responsibility of running the club and keeping it operational until the men returned. Actually, the public were not allowed to use the facilities at the pool until nearly 1920. It seems that during the four or five years that the bath had been used for the forces, considerable deterioration had set in. The fabric of the interior needed much attention and breakages required replacement. It was an expensive and time consuming period for the council.

The original builders were also criticised for poor workmanship with the discovery of roof leaks and holes in the balcony floor. This meant that a large sum of money had to be spent for necessary repairs. The structure of the pool was proved to have design faults too, for when the water was at its recommended level, the shallow end was too deep for small children to stand while learning to swim. To compensate for this, a stout wire was stretched the whole length of the pool from balcony to balcony, from shallow end to deep end, parallel to the pool edge and some 8 feet above it. Over this ran a pulley to which was attached a rope harness with comfortable rubber ringed armlets. Once the pupil was safe in these, the instructor could walk along the bathside supporting him and controlling the strokes and the pupil's fear of water. No doubt many Torbay residents will remember using this harness aid when they were being taught to swim at the Spa.

The bath was filled with sea-water directly from the adjacent Beacon Cove and in those early days heated to an unacceptable 65 degrees; far too cold for an indoor pool. There was one occasion, however, when through negligence, the water temperature rose to an alarming 84 degrees. This produced such a concentration of steam that visibility was reduced to a few yards and swimmers were imitating fog horn noises as they neared one another. On sunny days the large glass roof panels allowed the interior to be bathed in sunshine but this had an unpredictable drawback. After several days of fine weather the heat generated through the glass on to the salt water produced a growth of seaweed which clung firmly to the bath sides. This in turn required the pool being emptied far more often and a crew being employed in the laborious task of cleaning away this tenacious sea-plant. From the date of its opening the bath was emptied and refilled on the flood tide every so many days to keep the water as fresh and hygienic as possible. The filtration system was not introduced until 1934 when the 95,000 gallons of water was fully treated in a circulation turnover every three hours. Before the water entered the main filtration tank it had to pass through a colander sieve which captured any odds and ends discarded or lost by swimmers. It was quite remarkable the things that found their way into this latter unit: watches, wedding rings, engagement rings etc., but most of all false teeth.

A swimming bath superintendent's life is never dull. It is a constant saga of incidents, accidents, emergencies, tension and sometimes even tragedies. For him and his staff who are imprisoned within its echoing walls and subjected to the perpetual ear-splitting clamour of hundreds of over-excited screaming children, it can sometimes be very tiresome. Even worse when compounded by the sham screams of those pretending to be drowning. During its lifetime, the Spa swimming bath staff encountered a kaleidoscope of experiences, humorous, tragic, irresponsible or plainly absurd.

Vigilance was the key word in which every bather, whether child or adult, swimmer or non-swimmer, had to be considered as a possible drown-ee, and it was the responsibility of the superintendent to see that every bather who walked in – walked out.

An extraordinary accident happened in the swimming bath in 1930 resulting in national headlines in the leading newspapers. It was in fact the most astounding story in swimming bath history. A girl swimmer was sucked through the outlet pipe into the sea. To everyone's astonishment she survived the terrible ordeal. One could almost say it was a modern miracle. A detailed account of this incident follows later in this book.

Beacon Cove beach in 1935.

High tide, a sunny day and a crowded beach at the adjoining Beacon Cove in the 1930s. A view of the Marine Spa showing the large arched windows of the swimming bath, and high on the left, the windows of the ballroom.

During the period following the end of the First World War, the swimming club's successes were predominately in the ladies section, for the male members had hardly returned from France. Unfortunately however, in 1924, the club was in financial difficulties. They had to find money from some source to survive and decided to hold a dance upstairs in the great room which had been used for a variety of activities including roller skating. This however, had made the floor scarred and rough, quite unsuitable for dancing. Having hired the room for the occasion, members arrived with buckets and mops and scrubbed the whole floor. This done they then rubbed down the surface with sandstone and finished the job with a rotating polisher. The dance that followed was such a success and so rewarding they promoted another. However, when the Council saw how popular the idea was, they put a stop to 'room hire' and advertised their own dances. It was from this effort of the Leander Club that the former skating rink was permanently converted into the Spa ballroom and thus it remained until the whole complex was demolished in 1971.

SPECIAL ATTRACTIONS
Week Commencing 18th August. 1930

"DORIS & RALPH MOODY"
THE PREMIER BALLROOM DANCERS
IN A
SENSATIONAL & ARTISTIC
DANCE FANTASY

Do not fail to see England's most brilliant Dancing Couple in a Series of Dance Divertisements including demonstrations of the very latest developments in Modern Ballroom Dancing for 1930-1931

TABLES RESERVED   TELEPHONE 2172

The advertisement introduces the renowned national dancing partners Doris and Ralph Moody who attracted large crowds to the Spa during the 1930s.

Afternoon tea dances were regular features during the 1930s and 1940s. It was here many friendships blossomed into courtships and eventual marriage.

THE DEVON ARTS BALL

In January 1931, the Devon Art Society held its first Fancy Dress Ball at the Marine Spa. There were many excellent costumes and the function was greatly enjoyed by everyone. The Mayor and Mayoress (Councillor and Mrs F.W.Pratt) were present. The members of Ronald Rae's New Metro dance band straight from the Kit Kat Club, London, were dressed as scholars each wearing jerseys and little red caps, while Ronald Rae himself appeared complete with mortar board, gown and side whiskers. During the evening the band performed a 'novelty turn' with all the scholars leaving the room to return on either a bicycle, a scooter, a fairy cycle or roller skates. The drummer on skates lost control and crashed into the bandstand with such force it brought down several music stands and the cymbals.

The unrehearsed incident was rather like a pantomime, creating so much chaos amid roars of laughter from the onlookers it was some time before the dance could continue. Asked what he thought of the Ball, the mayor said, "I've never seen anything like it in Torquay in all my life, we should have a lot more of this sort of thing". It was not clear whether he was referring to the Ball or the skating incident.

One of the Spa's great nights to be remembered nearly seventy years ago when the Devon Arts Ball attracted over 400 guests.

Two of the most popular bands of those blessed memory days at the Spa were Art Jennings and Bob Roberts resident twenty piece bands. Their social grace and cordiality was unchallengeable.

The frequent morning concert in the Ballroom was a source of highly appreciative entertainment, many of which were broadcast by the B.B.C.

The magnificent Spa Ballroom. The bandstand was normally sited at the right-hand side of the room but as shown in this picture it had been moved to the far end to accommodate the famous Ivy Benson's All Women's Band.

The Spa Ballroom during a Grand Dancing Championship in the late 1930s. The dance band is believed to be Art Jennings' orchestra with himself as saxophonist.

The handsome foyer leading into the spacious Spa Ballroom for evening dances, morning concerts and afternoon tea dances.

In the years prior to its extinction, the ballroom became the mecca for vast numbers of people and for great occasions, special concerts and conferences. The main attraction was centred on the dance events where the music of famous London bands drifted out to fill the night air along the promenades. Often the ballroom was filled to capacity with couples swaying to the music of optimum bands like those of Ted Heath, Henry Hall and Victor Sylvester. The walls, floor and ceiling throbbed and pulsated to the reverberation of cornet and trumpet, saxophone and cymbal, of trombone and clarinet.

Quality musical programmes were a speciality of the Spa with high-class dance music. It was the hall-mark of entertainment in this beautifully sprung maple-floor ballroom which could accommodate over four-hundred dancers. Additionally, a dance hostess was permanently retained for the regular Tea and Evening Dances. Prices for admission were always very moderate: two shillings for tea and evening dances which included free parking.

Although the fox-trot and the waltz never lost their places among the popular dance routines of the time, it must be said the crazy gyrations of the Charleston, the Savanah Shuffle and the Black Bottom were top of the dance charts. The Spa became a meeting place, a centre, and many a romance budding from the Spa ballroom music led to the chime of wedding bells. Sequin spangled headbands with feathers, bright knee-length fringed dresses with ropes of multi-coloured beads, and the arrival of the smoking craze with long cigarette holders were hallmarks of the 1920s flapper. Bright young things expressed themselves in a high-pitched pseudo drawl and everybody was 'darling'. The mood was false and transitory, deceiving themselves into thinking they were having a hell of a good time with endless cocktails and inane laughter while they adopted the maxim 'live for today'. In a way it was understandable for the country was still recovering from the terrible slaughter of the First World War. Millions had been killed while still in their prime. The flower of the country's manhood decimated. "So" they argued, "why not live life to the full and enjoy every moment?".

As a result of Berkeley Hollyer's enterprise and business acumen, in January 1934 he secured the engagement of the world famous Billy Cotton's Dance Band. This was not only a great band but one of lively entertainment. At that time it was the most celebrated band that had ever played at the Spa. With its saxophones, trumpeting fanfares, blaring trombones and crashing cymbals it was certainly the noisiest. None of the occupants of the nearby Beacon Hill properties could ever have found any peace until well after midnight. The haunting tunes of *Let's Face the Music and Dance*, *Stormy Weather*, *Hi, Yi, Yi*, music from *Broadway Melody* such as *The Wedding of the Painted Doll* and *The Lullaby of Broadway*, compelled couples to join hundreds of others gyrating and whirling on the dance floor. The room became alive, bursting with the fun of the occasion.

At the time of the Jubilee of King George V, hundreds came to the Spa to dance to the rhythm of the great Lew Stone's band. It was a special event with the ballroom beautifully decorated in patriotic colours of red, white and blue. During the evening everyone attending was given a commemorative plated matchbox case. When one considers that the ticket price for these special occasions varied from only five shillings to eight shillings it seems incredible how the Spa ever met expenses. The administrative side of the Spa complexity of operations was conducted by only three people at any one time. Berkeley Hollyer as manager and publicity officer, Elsie Lamacraft as secretary and Phylis White as stenographer. Later Miss Grist (Mrs Gay) occupied the position of secretary.

Phylis White (1936) at the balustrade overlooking Beacon Cove.

One of Hollyer's most successful innovations was to introduce free entry for residents and visitors alike to the sun lounge. The revenue from refreshments served exceeded all expectations. The ballroom was given a new look and the floor regularly scrubbed every morning by a Mrs Harley who had the unenviable task of trying to scrub as much floor space as possible in two hours. For this exhausting labour she was paid the rate of two shillings and sixpence per hour. On one occasion because of a little extra time she gave, she earned an additional shilling. However, it seems the extra shilling carried her wage to just over the tax earning limit and thus into a tax category. The penalty for this was a tax deduction of two shillings. There was a near staff revolt over this but nothing came of it.

Tea and evening dances continued to grow in popularity and were well supported by Hotelier's Associations, Police Balls and limitless numbers of large clubs. Demonstrations by professional ballroom dancers from London and many Dance Championships for Amateurs attracted large crowds. Ronald Rae's dance orchestra remained one of the favourite bands for these special occasions.

THE TORQUAY ROWING CLUB.

Upon the break-up of the Haldon Estates in 1885, the Bath's Saloon complex was purchased by the then Local Government Board, later, the Town Council. The old swimming bath under the Bath's Saloons was, as seen in the photograph open to the sea through four spacious arches, often subjected to storm conditions and quite dark and sunless. The picture below shows the arches of the old swimming bath taken from Haldon Pier. After it was abandoned as a swimming bath, the Torquay Rowing Club took it over in 1869, covering the pool area with firm boards and using it as their permanent headquarters.

This fine picture taken at the turn of the century shows the four arches leading into the Torquay Rowing Club's headquarters which, until 1869, housed the old swimming bath. Above the four arches can be seen the impressive and spacious viewing terrace. Dominating this is the structure of the famous ballroom, while away to the right is the monumental Imperial Hotel with its original facade. From the number of spectators to the left of the picture and the several nearby waiting boats, it appears to be the advent of a gala occasion.

The Torquay Rowing Club had a large following in those days with its crews competing in and winning many championships in county events. Its fifth President was Lord of the Manor of Cockington, Richard Mallock who maintained his presidency from 1891 to 1900.

This very old photograph dated 1876 shows one of their winning crews. Names are left to right: Austin, Day, Heas and MacMillan. The cox is Shapley, possibly of the Shapley family business on the Strand.

The Torquay Rowing Club champion team of 1896, proudly displaying a collection of valuable trophies won in that competitive season. Names left to right are F. Salte, W. Netherway, W. Airey, L. Pook, and C. Pridham. The Cox in the foreground is E. Brown, who was to have a distinguished future. His appointments included Secretary of State for Scotland 1941; Minister of Health 1941–1943; Minister of Aircraft Production 1945. On his retirement he was made a Companion of Honour.

The 1897 Torquay Carnival procession proceeding down Union St in May of that year. Celebrating Queen Victoria's Diamond Jubilee a heavy horse-drawn dray carries a champion Torquay Rowing Club crew and their boat, just passing the entrance to Market Street.

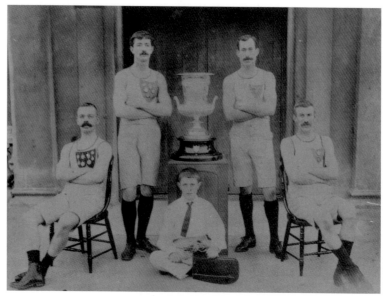

The club's 1899 Senior Championship crew proudly showing their winning trophy – the West of England Challenge Cup.
The crew left to right: W. Netherway, L. Pook, E. Warne and A. Heywood. In the foreground is the Cox, W. Tregaskis.

1900, the christening of the club's new boat 'Mabel' after Mrs Mabel Struben. Inside these four arches is the site of the old swimming bath which by this time had been covered with strong boards. It was on this large surface that the club's boats were housed. Above the arches can be seen a part of the Bath's Saloons building adjacent to the medical section.

The Senior Champion crew of 1905 posing for a photograph close to headquarters. Beyond is the Millstone and in the distance, units of the Home Fleet. Between the club boat and the Millstone is a swimmers running board platform with a convenient raft on the right. The crew is W. Burridge (Stroke), R. Reed, W. Netherway, S. Carter and W. Bailey (Cox).

1908, the christening of the club's new boat 'Stella', performed by Mrs Stella Luxmore, wife of a founder member. The new boat lies grandly on the ramp between the arches and Haldon Pier.

A fine sunny day in 1924 for the launching of another new club boat, the 'Lady Betty'. On the left is the ramp leading to Haldon Pier with a goodly crowd of members watching from inside the arches of the old swimming bath.

A splendid aerial view of the Marine Spa complex showing the adjacent Beacon Cove, Haldon Pier, Beacon Terrace, The Strand, the Pavilion and Torquay's long sea front.

A rare photograph of the interior of the Torquay Rowing Club's headquarters at the Marine Spa taken in 1947 showing the boarded floor covering the old swimming bath which still held three feet of sea-water. The picture shows the club's ladies and junior crews with their championship trophies.
Back row left to right: Miss A. Gerard, Miss B. Weeks, Miss E. Crocker, J. Heale, J. Webster, C. Natley, E. Claydon.
Middle row left to right: Mrs E. Bindon, Mrs W. Strancer, Miss R. Pringle, K. Ireland, G. Dunn, R. Pringle.
Front row left to right: Miss D. Hogarth, Miss E. Pick, Mr A. Adams, (President) F.Clark (Chairman), W. Peek, E. Barrow and sitting, forefront - M.Ferrigno.

The Torquay Rowing Club's Ladies Champions of 1969. Left to right: Miss M. Gatting, Miss M. Jackson, Mrs P. Glanfield (Ladies President), Miss P. Bird, Miss W. Williams and Miss C. Patch.

Torbay, at a time when the water was in capricious mood and not an ideal day for the Torquay Rowing Club's slim skiffs to practice, but ideal conditions for the visiting Tall Ships pictured above during 1975.

The Bath's Saloons complex during the early 1900s.

The floodlit Bath's Saloons.

APPREHENSION OVER THE SWIMMING BATH AND THE
UNFORTUNATE EVENTS PRECEDING ITS DEMOLITION

It was in 1963 that the first rumblings of disquiet were heard when Council officials began to voice their misgivings about the condition of the Spa Swimming Bath. In a report dated January 1964, the then Local Medical Officer of Health Dr E. MacTaggart, stated that there were many aspects in which the bath fell short of standards of health, safety and convenience.

A few years later, following an inspection by Torquay's Chief Architect, Mr Banks, it was also declared that the foundations and lower walls were giving cause for concern and three large steel girders had to be positioned across the width of the bath to support the outer wall which was gradually moving inward. Additionally, other signs of decay and general deterioration were plainly visible. As a result, expert opinion came to the reluctant conclusion that the bath could not be saved; it was dangerous and would have to be demolished. The council were not quite sure when, but in 1971, the decision was taken out of their hands by the ghastly tragedy of an eleven year old boy who was sucked through the narrow filtration pipe in the bottom of the bath; an accident which seemed virtually impossible.

The Spa swimming bath had not been without its misfortunes and tragedies. On the 1st September,1930 a girl swimmer was sucked feet first through 150 feet of the outlet pipe from the bath and finally deposited into the sea, fortunately into shallow water. Amazingly, she survived the ordeal, her escape becoming world news.

The event occurred at a time when for cleaning purposes the bath had to be emptied. This operation involved a massive volume of water flowing into and through a circular vent in the end wall which gave access to a 10 inch inside diameter iron pipe with its outfall some distance away in Beacon Cove.

But how and why did this nightmare experience happen. Rumour current at the time was that the bath attendant after checking there were no swimmers in the pool opened the outlet valve, unaware that a young girl swimmer was still on the top diving board. Minutes later, the girl, 15 years old Phyllis Bastin, took a last dive before dressing. This it was claimed brought her in line with the pipe and the suction created by 90,000 gallons of water rushing into a small aperture sucked her through it.

Seventy years have passed since that story circulated but now the true details have emerged in an article from an old Torquay Times (recently discovered), dated 12th September 1930, which gives the full account recently confirmed by Phylis Bastin herself (Mrs Williams) who survived the terrible ordeal. The report in the Torquay Times in Sept 1930 carried the heading –

GIRL'S ACCIDENT AT THE BATHS – A SENSATIONAL INTERVIEW.

"We received no warning whatsoever that there was any danger at the deep-end and there are about six or seven people in the party who can verify that statement"

These words were stated in the course of an interview with a member of the party who were bathing with Miss Bastin when she was drawn down the 10 inch pipe from the Baths into the sea. This gentleman, who probably saw more of the accident than anyone else, described the whole of the unfortunate affair to our representative yesterday.

"A party of us went from the Roslin Hotel to the Baths at about 12.30pm. On arrival at the Box office we saw a young lady who told us they were emptying the bath but that it would not be completely empty for another 20 minutes, so we got our tickets and went into the water. While we were in the water we could see that it was going down because it was only about five feet deep at the deepest point of the bath. When the water had gone down to about two or three feet in the deepest point, I was talking to Miss Bastin. I half-turned away and at the same time I heard Miss Bastin make some exclamation and as I turned round, her head was disappearing under the surface and her hands were in the air as if she was trying to catch hold of me. I shouted for the attendant for some time but he was a long time coming. He told me after a lot of argument where the pipe came out and we ran down to the beach. We put her in the car and I drove her to Torbay Hospital. So far from being warned to keep to the shallow end, everybody was at the deep end and there was no attendant in sight to warn us of the danger."

Phyllis spent several months in hospital recovering from severe blood poisoning. At the time, doctors feared she might die from the effects of her near death experience. "I was in a terrible state" she recalled, "the rust and barnacles inside the pipe scraped off the skin giving lacerations right down to the bone. When the accident happened I felt my feet being dragged into the hole and cried out. Fortunately, I took a deep breath just before going under and this allowed me to hold out. I was conscious throughout the experience; if I had not been I doubt if I would have survived. When I popped up in the sea, covered in blood, a lady nearby had quite a shock. I was helped up the beach and then driven to Torbay Hospital by a friend".

While in hospital she received hundreds of letters including a proposal of marriage from a man in Italy. Phyllis had come to Torquay on holiday with her parents from Buckinghamshire. She was a keen tennis player and one of her few lasting regrets is that the accident prevented her competing in junior Wimbledon for which she had qualified in 1930.

She remembers another incident clearly. When she recovered consciousness she received an unexpected visitor in the person of one of King George V's

physicians, Sir Farquhar Buzzard K.C.V.O., M.D. who was holidaying in Torquay at the time. The following year, at his request, she visited him at his consulting rooms in London where he congratulated her on her wonderful recovery from such serious injuries and expressed the opinion that he never believed it possible for anyone to survive the chronic septicaemia which had resulted.

Some period later, following a redevelopment, the old outlet vent in the end wall was replaced by a small vent in the bath floor at the deep end over

Phyllis Bastin (now Mrs Phyllis Williams) now living near Dartmoor.

which two strong steel bars were secured. The authorities were convinced that a similar accident could never happen again. How wrong they were!

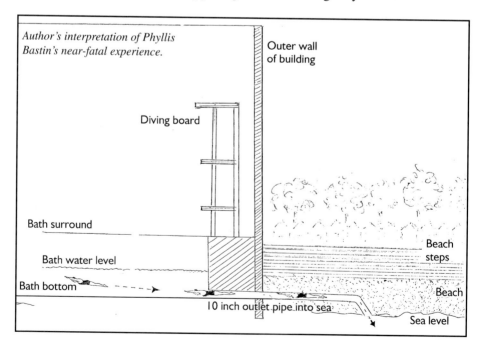

Author's interpretation of Phyllis Bastin's near-fatal experience.

Outer wall of building

Diving board

Bath surround

Beach steps

Bath water level

Bath bottom

Beach

10 inch outlet pipe into sea

Sea level

The following photograph of Beacon Cove in 1935 shows the outlet pipe sloping towards the sea through which Phyllis Bastin was drawn. Now Mrs Phyllis Williams, she married in 1936 and after being widowed, moved to a town near Dartmoor where she now enjoys retirement with her hobbies as a keen artist and craftswoman, though still with fleeting memories of that traumatic event of seventy years ago.

No tragic accident occurred at the Spa swimming bath during the next eight years but between April 1937 and June 1938 two male swimmers died from heart attacks in the pool. Both middle aged and well-known personalities in Torquay, they were seemingly in good health. These sad events cast a spell of gloom over the activities of the Spa for some time but with the coming of war in 1939 the Spa tragedies were overtaken by the national call-to-arms.

On the evening of the 13th July 1971, three children from St Vincent's Children's Home were in the baths enjoying a swimming session. One of these was eleven years old John Moran who with other boys was diving in and out of the pool from the bathside. This, so one story goes, developed into a more daring game as to who could stay longest sitting on the bottom. At eight o'clock the attendant closed the session and ordered all swimmers to dress. Quite soon it was discovered that John was missing and the alarm raised when his clothes were found in a cubicle. He certainly could not have left the building naked and therefore had to be in the pool. Immediately, Torbay Fire Brigade were called to empty the 90,000 gallons of water while divers from the Torquay Sub-aqua Club made efforts to locate the body which could only be in the outlet pipe. Using torches, they could see John's feet but were unable to attach a rope to them.

With police and council officials present, men with pneumatic drills worked

throughout the night and the following day in an effort to recover the body which meant demolishing part of the end wall of the bath.

The foremost question that arose was how could the boy have got into the 10 inch interior diameter pipe? One solution put forward was that John actually sat on the outlet vent of the pipe for a few seconds where the gentle withdrawal of water induced by the power pump in the circulation system, (now plugged by the obstruction) built up into an energy force of suction from which there was no escape and growing stronger with every moment that passed. Within seconds that power had developed such strength that the body was sucked through.

Probably the last photograph of John Moran, taken shortly before his tragic death.

No blame could be attributed to anyone. It was an ever present lurking danger that never revealed itself until it actually happened. John was due to start at Cuthbert Mayne Roman Catholic Secondary School in Torquay in September after leaving Abbey Road Roman Catholic Primary School at the end of that term. The circumstances of John's death at the Marine Spa had its repercussions throughout Torbay and even now, thirty years on, proposals have been put forward to create a complex development on the former Marine Spa site as a memorial to young John Moran.

Early on the morning of the 27th September, 1971, a giant bulldozer clamourously trundled its way into the empty Torquay Marine Spa car-park, shattering the peaceful aura that brooded over the place. The few people around were mainly dog-walkers and early rising holiday visitors but plainly visible, a few council workmen with their foreman.

Advancing like an enemy tank with its articulated tracks biting into the tarmac, it paused before the gracious portal leading to the magnificent foyer within and began its brutal destructive mission. The long hydraulic powered arm rose high above the facing wall and there hung menacingly over its target while the talon toothed head was positioned for its first deadly strike.

At a nod from the foreman, the driver pulled a small lever and with a jarring crash the massive steel crown fell upon the roof-top. Like a prehistoric monster devouring its prey the steel jaws closed around the stone and timbered structure which for a century and more had so loyally played its part in maintaining the dignity of this noble building. A sickening tearing sound rent the air as the arm pulled clear with wall and roofing fabric dripping from its sabre-toothed mouth.

Thus began the rape of Torquay's most beautiful and enchanting architectural establishment which, in its one hundred years had emerged from early embryonic stage, through puberty to adulthood, blossoming into a mecca of pleasure and entertainment for thousands of residents and visitors alike.

Through its spacious palmed entrance had passed dukes and diplomats, stage and screen stars and every race colour and creed. But now the famous Torquay Marine Spa, this outstanding edifice which dwelt with so much affection in the hearts and minds of the people of Torbay was, by order of the Council being ripped apart piece by piece. To many, by the demolition of this lovely building it seemed as though the very social heart of Torquay was being torn out. As the hours passed on that long remembered day the crowd of bystanders grew dramatically. The news had spread fast and although there was no militancy, one could not ignore the ubiquitous resentful atmosphere that prevailed. Despite the heartrending noise of the demolition, expressions of 'shame', 'it's wicked', 'but why?', were clearly heard. But the driver of the mechanical destructor neither heard nor cared. He had a job to do and was doing it well. By noon that day the clawed arm of the great juggernaut had torn deep into the walls and roof of the administration offices to the right of the main entrance.

Later the bulldozer swung left on its merciless mission, the long arm lifting high to claw savagely at the elaborately decorated ceiling of the spacious foyer. Within minutes an avalanche of steel girders, plastered panelling and iron stanchions came hurtling down in a sickening crash amid a cloud of dust and debris. Many years ago, here in this grand vestibule, elegant gowned ladies and white tie and black tailed gentlemen greeted one another before making their entry into the music filled ballroom.

And so the demolition went on, week after week, the ravishing of Torquay's hallowed palace of memories. When the dust finally settled, all that remained was a pyramid of debris, a monument to man's skill at demolition. Thirty years have passed since those days and although the rubble has been cleared, all that can now be seen on what must be one of Torbay's most geographically prime and valuable sites, is a derilect, scarred wasteland, while beyond it lies Torbay's glorious bay; one in direct disassociation with the other. Here displayed for all to see is a panoramic spectacle of desolation lying side by side with nature's intoxicating beauty.

THE RAPE OF THE QUEEN OF THE ENGLISH RIVIERA

A sorrowful day in Torquay history, September 1971.